SO-ELF-553

TIME
CHRONICLES

The
Strange
Box

Written by Roderick Hunt
and illustrated by Alex Brychta

OXFORD
UNIVERSITY PRESS

Introduction

A long time has passed since the children have been on a magic key adventure. In fact, they have almost forgotten the last time the key glowed.

Biff and Chip are now ten, Kipper is eight, and Wilma has started secondary school.

When Chip discovers a strange old box in his room, things begin to change forever.

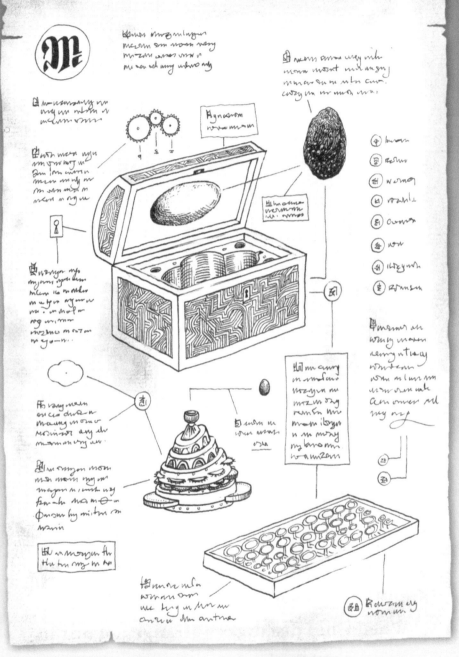

The Parts of the TimeWeb

"The TimeWeb is an ancient machine. It acts like an eye looking into the past ... See, it has four parts; the Hub ... the Matrix ... the Cell ... and the box is the case which connects it all together."

Chapter 1

Chip found the old box on top of his wardrobe. It had been there for years. He'd just forgotten about it.

He took the box down, blew the dust off, and looked at it curiously.

"Come and see this, Biff," he called.

The box was made of heavy metal and had strange markings on it.

"We found the magic key inside it," said Chip. "Do you remember?" He scratched the lid with his finger-nail.

"It's rusty," Biff said. "But the rust is an odd, green colour."

They took the box downstairs and Biff rubbed it with a scouring pad. Under the green rust, the metal shone with different colours.

"It looks like oil when it's spilled on water," said Biff.

Kipper came into the kitchen. He flung his football kit on the floor, went to the fridge and poured himself a glass of orange juice.

"Hey! What a weird-looking box," he said.

"It had the magic key in it," replied Chip, "but it's not much use. The inside is all peculiar. Look!"

The box was empty, but inside were metal grooves and slots. It looked as if something complicated had once fitted exactly into it.

"We've no idea what it is, or what it was used for," said Biff.

Chip left the box on the worktop and they all went upstairs.

What they didn't see was the faint glow that seeped out through the half-shut lid of the box.

Chapter 2

The big event of the weekend was the school fair. The money raised at the fair was going to buy IT equipment.

Mum had been busy making cakes to sell. Biff, Chip and Kipper had filled a bag with old toys and games for the toy stall.

That Saturday, Wilma's mum came to the house to collect things for her second-hand stall. Wilma was helping her to run it.

"We've not much for you," said Mum. "There's a vase, some china cats and a picture that none of us likes."

Chip spotted the old box on the worktop. "How about this? Somebody might want to buy it," he said. He looked at Biff and Kipper. "We don't want it, do we?"

Biff and Kipper shook their heads.

And so Wilma's mum took the box to sell on her stall.

After that, the trouble began.

Chapter 3

Later the family went to the supermarket.
When they got home, Floppy was
barking loudly. A window had been broken
and the kitchen door was open.

"Someone's broken in," gasped Dad.

"Oh no!" exclaimed Mum. "What have
they taken?"

They looked round to see what had been stolen, but nothing was missing.

The only strange thing was that the house felt very cold, and the glass from a broken light bulb lay on the floor.

"Maybe Floppy saw them off," said Biff.

"It's very odd," thought Chip. "I wonder what they were after?"

Later, Biff called Chip to her room.

"I know this sounds silly," she began, "but do you think it was a good idea to give the old box away? We did find the key in it."

"Why not? The key's still safe, isn't it?"

Biff opened a drawer where the key was hidden in a pair of her old socks.

"Of course it is," she said.

Chapter 4

Wilma found it strange to be back in her old school. Last year she had moved up to the secondary school.

Now she was back helping her mum to run a stall at the school fair.

She enjoyed setting up the stall. She put large objects at the back, and smaller ones at the front.

She had a surprise when she picked up the
old box.

"It's really heavy," she said.

In the end, she put the box next to a brass
dish and the china cats.

Wilma's mum was on a separate table. She
was selling the more valuable items.

Everyone was pleased to see Mrs May at the fair. She had retired two years ago and had come back to open it.

"I want you all to spend lots of money," joked Mrs May, "and make this the best school fair ever. I now declare the fair open."

People rushed to the stalls to try and get a bargain. On Wilma's stall many of the items sold quickly, but nobody seemed interested in the old box.

Then something strange happened. It felt as if an icy wind had blown through the hall. Then there was a loud pop. One of the strip lights had exploded. Then the lights flickered and went dim.

"A power cut," someone groaned.

Mr Mortlock, the caretaker, hurried into the hall, but then the lights came back on again.

"How odd!" said Wilma's mum.

Chapter 5

Nadim came to the stall with Wilf and Neena. He picked up the old box and opened it.

"I like this, Wilma. How much?" he asked.

"Five pounds?" replied Wilma hopefully.

"Fine," said Nadim, handing Wilma the money.

"But I'd like to buy that box, too," said a voice behind them.

Nadim spun round. The voice was icy and sinister. It belonged to a tall man in a long coat. He had pale, waxy skin, bright green eyes and very black hair.

The man's eyes were so cold and piercing that Wilma shuddered.

"I'm sorry, the box is sold," she said, even though the man scared her.

The man stared at Nadim. "I'll give you thirty pounds. That's six times what you paid for it," he said.

Nadim imagined that if a snake could talk, its voice would sound just like this man's. But something made Nadim want to keep the box, whatever the man offered him, so he shook his head.

"You stupid boy," the man hissed. "You have no use for the box. But I have. All right, I'll give you fifty pounds."

Biff and Chip gasped. Fifty pounds was a lot for a useless old box.

"Take the money," urged Chip.

Out of the corner of his eye, Nadim saw Mr Mortlock shaking his head.

Nadim's heart beat fast. It was hard to breathe. He thought what he could do with fifty pounds, but something told him not to sell the box to this man.

"Sorry," he said. "It's not for sale."

The man opened his mouth to speak, but Mr Mortlock moved close to Nadim.

"Is everything all right?" Mr Mortlock asked in a firm voice.

The man stared at Nadim with lizard-like eyes. They made the hair rise on the back of Nadim's neck.

"Er...yes," said Nadim. "I think so."

The man turned sharply and strode away. Mr Mortlock spoke quietly to himself.

"So, the enemy has come!" he said.

Chapter 6

Every Saturday afternoon Biff, Chip and Kipper took Floppy for a walk. They ran home quickly and put Floppy on his lead. Then they walked back to school to meet their friends.

They wanted to talk about the scary man. Who was he? Why did he want the box so badly, and what did Mr Mortlock have to do with it?

They met up with Wilf, Wilma, Nadim and Neena outside the school.

As they walked home together, Chip noticed that Nadim was holding the old box tightly under his arm.

They all talked about the sinister man who had come to the stall. The thought of him made them shudder.

"Ugh! That weird man who wanted to buy that box ..." Wilma began.

Chip cut in. "But you turned down fifty pounds, Nadim," he said. "I would have taken the money just to get rid of him."

Nadim shrugged. "There was something about him. I couldn't let him have it."

Suddenly Floppy stopped and growled.

"Has it turned chilly?" asked Kipper.

Then, as they turned into the park, there he was – the strange man. He was standing in front of them, blocking their way.

"I want that box," he hissed. "It is not yours, it's mine. Give it to me."

Chip's heart gave a leap. "It was you who broke into our house," he shouted. "You were looking for the box."

But the man just stared at Nadim.

Nadim felt he couldn't turn away from
the cold gaze of the man's green eyes. He
held the box out, and the man's gloved hand
reached out to take it.

"No!" shouted Biff. She snatched the box
away just as the gloved fingers closed on it.
The man lunged at her, but she threw the
box back to Nadim.

"Run!" shouted Biff.

They ran in a group, Nadim in the middle with the box under his arm. As if from nowhere, the man was in front of them.

"That's impossible," gasped Wilf.

The man stretched out his arms as if he was pulling them towards him.

Behind them came the sound of running footsteps. It was Mr Mortlock.

He stood in front of the man and pointed something at him.

There was a bright flash and a loud, crackling sound.

The man dissolved into a green flame that curled and twisted into a serpent-like shape.

Then, like a firework, the shape turned into sparks and tiny shards of flame. They shot into the air, with a hiss and a whoosh.

"The time has come sooner than I wanted," shouted Mr Mortlock. "The enemy is here, but we still have the box. Run, all of you. Run through the door."

It was as if a shimmering heat haze had risen in front of the trees. In the centre of it was a blue door.

"It's a door in the landscape," gasped Chip. "It's like the one in the magic key adventures."

The door swung open. There was only one thing to do ...

... they ran through it.

Now what?

What will the children find on the other side of the door? Are they in danger?

Who was the strange man and why did he want the box so badly?

How could the man simply disappear in a shower of sparks? Was he a human?

And who is Mr Mortlock? Why did he say, "So the enemy has come"? What did he mean?

Find out in the next book:
Beyond the Door
There isn't a moment to lose!

Chip

School: Ortree Primary

Age: 10   *Year:* 6

Likes: art

Dislikes: quarrelling

Special ability: sense of humour

Kipper

School: Ortree Primary

Age: 8   *Year:* 4

Likes: reading

Dislikes: finishing things

Special ability: telling jokes

Biff

School: Ortree Primary

Age: 10   *Year:* 6

Likes: making things

Dislikes: wearing skirts

Special ability: reliable and brave

Wilf

School: Ortree Primary

Age: 10   *Year:* 6

Likes: skateboarding

Dislikes: being bossed around

Special ability: acting and
                        performing

Neena

School: Ortree Primary
Age: 11   *Year*: 6
Likes: making music
Dislikes: swimming
Special ability: being helpful

Nadim

School: Ortree Primary
Age: 11   *Year*: 6
Likes: gadgets and computers
Dislikes: singing
Special ability: solving problems

Wilma

School: Walton High School
Age: 12   *Year*: 7
Likes: nice clothes
Dislikes: mess
Special ability: common sense

Floppy

School: Obedience Training
Age: 12   *Dog years*: 84
Likes: sleeping
Dislikes: baths
Special ability: loyal and
                   protective

Glossary

exclaimed *(page 14)* Shouted or cried out in excitement or surprise. *"Oh no!" exclaimed Mum. "What have they taken?"*

lunged *(page 32)* Moved forward quickly and suddenly. *The man lunged at her …*

piercing *(page 23)* A piercing stare makes you feel as if the person can see right into your mind. It is a very uncomfortable feeling. *The man's eyes were so cold and piercing that Wilma shuddered.*

seeped *(page 10)* Oozed out slowly (usually used about light or water). *What they didn't see was the faint glow that seeped out through the half-shut lid of the box.*

serpent *(page 34)* Another word for a snake. *The man dissolved into a green flame that curled and twisted into a serpent-like shape.*

sinister *(page 29)* Something that is scary or threatening. *They all talked about the sinister man who had come to the stall.*

valuable *(page 18)* Something of great value – usually either worth a lot of money or of great personal importance. *Wilma's mum … was selling the more valuable items.*

Thesaurus: Another word for …
sinister *(page 29)* menacing, intimidating, threatening, ominous.